WEAPONS AND MACHINES IN WARFARE

WEAPONS AND MACHINES OF THE VIETNAM WAR

Craig Boutland

Cavendish Square

Published in 2024 by Cavendish Square Publishing, LLC
2544 Clinton Street, Buffalo, NY 14224

Portions of this work were originally authored by Charlie Samuels and published as *Machines and Weaponry of the Vietnam War*. All new material this edition authored by Craig Boutland.

Website: cavendishsq.com

Design Manager: Keith Davis
Picture Manager: Sophie Mortimer

Picture Credits
Front Cover: U.S. Department of Defense
All photographs Library of Congress Except: Fly-By-Owen: 11b; Robert Hunt Library: 6, 10, 15br, 38; Shutterstock: Darren Brode 22, RCP Photo 15t; U.S. Department of Defense: 1, 8, 9tr, 32, 33, 36, 40, 41, 44.
Key: t = top, c = center, b = bottom, l = left, r = right.

Cataloging-in-Publication Data

Names: Boutland, Craig.
Title: Weapons and machines of the Vietnam War / Craig Boutland.
Description: Buffalo, New York : Cavendish Square Publishing, 2024. | Series: Weapons and machines in warfare | Includes glossary and index.
Identifiers: ISBN 9781502669209 (pbk.) | ISBN 9781502669216 (library bound) | ISBN 9781502669223 (ebook)
Subjects: LCSH: Vietnam War, 1961-1975--Equipment and supplies--Juvenile literature. | Vietnam War, 1961-1975--Technology--Juvenile literature. | Military weapons--History--20th century--Juvenile literature.
Classification: LCC DS559.8.S9 B66 2024 | DDC 959.704'34--dc23

CPSIA compliance information: Batch #CSCSQ24: For further information contact Cavendish Square Publishing LLC at 1-877-980-4450.

Printed in the United States of America

CONTENTS

U.S. Marines take shelter behind a partly destroyed wall during fighting for the central Vietnamese city of Hue.

Introduction

There was open warfare or low-level fighting in Southeast Asia from the 1940s to nearly the end of the 20th century. The most intense fighting was in Vietnam, which had been ruled as a colony by France up to World War II. After the war, Vietnamese **nationalists** defeated their French rulers. They set up an independent communist state in North Vietnam. The United States feared that communism might spread to South Vietnam and became involved in the region.

nationalists: People who believe in the right of a nation to govern itself.

UNEVEN TECHNOLOGY

Starting in 1961, U.S. military advisors arrived to help the Army of South Vietnam (ARVN). Ground troops arrived in March 1965. The Americans and their allies faced the Army of North Vietnam (NVA) and a **guerrilla** force based in the South, called the Viet Cong or VC.

On paper, U.S. forces were far superior to their enemy. However, the terrain was hostile, and the enemy were skilled in jungle fighting and guerrilla warfare. North Vietnam avoided defeat until public opinion at home forced a U.S. withdrawal. In 1975, the war finally ended when North Vietnamese troops defeated the ARVN and captured Saigon, capital of South Vietnam.

Phosphorus bombs explode among enemy positions in May 1966. One U.S. commander said that he wanted to bomb Vietnam "back to the Stone Age."

guerrilla: An irregular soldier who fights using ambush, sabotage, and assassination.

Skyraiders fly in formation on a mission above the flat landscape of the Mekong Delta in southern Vietnam.

A-1 Skyraider

Nicknamed "Spad" or "Able Dog" by its crew, the Douglas A-1 Skyraider first flew into action in 1945, at the end of World War II. When U.S. armed intervention in Vietnam began in 1961, Skyraiders were called into action. The intention was to use the plane as a **stopgap** and to replace it with more modern aircraft. Instead, it lasted the whole war. The Skyraider was tough, adaptable, and carried heavy weights. It attacked at low altitude, just above treetops, and often in the face of relentless anti-aircraft fire.

stopgap: A temporary fix for a problem.

A Skyraider releases a napalm bomb as it approaches a target thought to be used by the Viet Cong.

"ABLE DOG" MUNITIONS

The propeller-driven A-1 was only capable of a top speed of 318 miles per hour (512 km/h). However, it made up for being slow by being powerful. It could carry up to 8,000 pounds (3,270 kg) of bombs, **cluster bombs**, or chemicals such as napalm and phosphorus. It could also fire rockets and had two 20-mm cannons.

ODD BOMB

In October 1965, Commander Clarence W. Stoddard, Jr., used his A-1H Skyraider, Paper Tiger II, to drop an unusual load: a toilet. U.S. crews dropped it on North Vietnam to mark the six millionth pound of bombs to be dropped.

Another benefit of the Skyraider was its ability to stay airborne longer and fly longer distances than other aircraft in the war. That made it perfect for carrying out search-and-rescue missions to locate soldiers behind enemy lines.

Technicians load munitions beneath the wing of a Skyraider before a mission.

cluster bombs: Bombs that contain a number of "bomblets" that all detonate together.

A-4 Skyhawk

The Douglas A-4 Skyhawk flew more missions than any other U.S. naval aircraft during the Vietnam War. It was nicknamed the "Bantam Bomber" because of its light weight. Both the Marines and the Navy used versions of this compact **ground-attack aircraft**. Indeed, it was a Marine Skyhawk that dropped the last U.S. bombs of the war. It took off from aircraft carriers, so it didn't need land airstrips.

This Navy A-4 has been fitted with additional fuel tanks beneath the wings to increase its range.

ground-attack aircraft: A warplane used to attack targets on the ground.

HOT ROD

The light bomber was sometimes called "Heinemann's Hot Rod," for its designer, Ed Heinemann. He wanted the aircraft to be light and simple to use. He made it half the weight of other bombers. That meant it was easy to maneuver but also fast. It set an air-speed record in 1954 of 695 miles per hour (1,120 km/h).

A pilot prepares for a mission onboard an aircraft carrier. The planes' wings made them easy to store on carriers.

The planes had **delta wings**. They fit in the holds of aircraft carriers without having to be folded. Although it was light, the A-4 could carry up to 8,200 pounds (3,720 kg) of bombs.

A technician loads 20-mm ammunition for a Skyhawk's cannons.

EYEWITNESS

"I was off! Whoosh! It was like being shot from a sling. The initial surge pinned my head and body back against the seat. My eyeballs rattled and my vision blurred. . . This was more exhilarating than the heady plunge of a rocketing roller coaster."

Everett Alvarez, Jr.
1st U.S. pilot shot down in Vietnam

delta wing: A wing shaped like a swept-back triangle.

AC-47 Gunship

The AC-47 Gunship was the first in a series of heavily armed gunships used by the U.S. Air Force in Vietnam. It was a flying arsenal and bristled with weapons. Nicknamed "Spooky" or "Puff the Magic Dragon," the AC-47 first saw action in 1965. It was designed to give U.S. ground troops close support. One of its great advantages was that it could stay in the air for long periods, waiting for the call to help infantry formations.

A "Spooky" flies above Vietnam. The gunship's huge firing capacity could be used to fire flares to light up ground fighting at night.

arsenal: A place for storing weapons.

The guns were mounted in the rear windows of the gunship; they could all be controlled by the pilot.

Tracer fire lights up the sky as AC-47s attack targets in a Vietnamese city.

FIREPOWER

"Spooky" carried either three powerful **miniguns** or 10 machine guns, placed in the windows and a side door. The pilot could fire the guns all together or individually. The aircraft carried 24,000 rounds of ammunition.

It was said that a three-second burst of gunfire could put one round in every square foot of a target as big as a football field. Such firepower terrified the enemy.

EYEWITNESS

"Over time, Spooky was requested more and more frequently, and it required less and less time over the target to convince the VC fighters to quit and go home."

Bob Stein
AC-47 pilot

minigun: A multi-barreled machine gun that can fire 2,000 to 6,000 rounds a minute.

The Cobra carried rockets and bombs beneath its stub wings. It had a cannon mounted in a turret beneath the nose.

AH-1 Cobra

The jungles and mountains that covered much of Vietnam made it difficult to build airstrips for fixed-wing aircraft. Landing zones for helicopters were easier to create, and so Vietnam was called a "helicopter war." Known as the "HueyCobra" or the "Snake," the Bell AH-1 Cobra was developed soon after the war began as the first helicopter **gunship** developed to support troops in the frontline.

gunship: A heavily armed helicopter or airplane.

ESCORT CHOPPER

The Cobra was first used in response to the North Vietnamese Tet Offensive in 1968. From then until the end of the war, Cobras clocked over 1 million hours of flying time. About 300 of the 1,100 choppers were lost. Over the course of the war, their design was changed to minimize the chance of losses due to antiaircraft fire.

EYEWITNESS

"We flew much more reconnaissance than close air support, as we were the eyes of the division. We were always way out in front of our ground troops, looking for targets for them to exploit."

Chief Warrant Officer Randy Zhan
Commander, Cindy Ann Cobra

The job of the Cobra was to provide **fire support** for ground forces and to escort transport helicopters. As soldiers dropped to the ground, they were at risk of attack. The Cobra hovered close by. Its two multibarreled guns, seven rockets, and 20-mm cannon provided cover for the infantry.

A technician loads 70-mm Folding Fin Aerial Rockets (FFARs) onto a Cobra.

Cobras fly in formation low over the Vietnamese forest. Although heavily armed, they were vulnerable to antiaircraft fire.

fire support: Providing additional or covering fire for forces on the ground.

AK-47

In 1942, Sergeant Mikhail Kalashnikov of the Soviet Union Army designed a new gun. His designs finally came to fruition in 1949. The new weapon was dubbed the AK-47, and it became the most successful **assault rifle** ever devised. In Vietnam, some U.S. soldiers preferred the AK-47 to their own M16 rifles. If they captured an AK-47, they often kept it and used it.

These AK-47s are part of a weapons hoard that was seized by U.S. troops during operations in South Vietnam.

assault rifle: An automatic or semiautomatic gun that can hold many rounds of ammunition.

A POPULAR RIFLE

The AK-47 was cheap to produce and very reliable. It was easy to maintain. It worked well even in the steamy jungles of Vietnam, where other guns often jammed. The gun was small and light, and comfortable enough to carry on long marches.

The AK-47 was an automatic: This meant it fired continuously when the trigger was squeezed. A firing rate of 600 rounds per minute enabled any target to be **raked** with fire. Over 100 million AK-47s have been manufactured, and the weapon is still in use today.

RIFLE WARFARE

Most of the time, Vietnam was not a high-tech war. Much of the fighting was done by infantry at close quarters, so the soldier's best friend was his rifle. It had to be reliable and close by. Whether crawling through tunnels or hacking through the jungle, a soldier always had to have his gun at the ready.

This member of the Viet Cong holds his AK-47 as he stands on top of a destroyed U.S. personnel carrier.

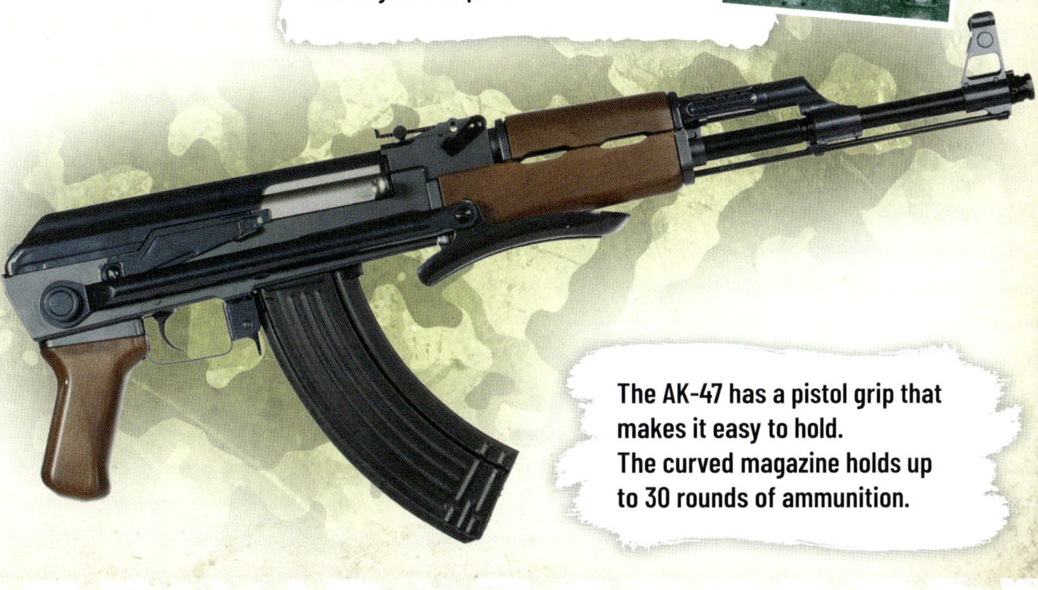

The AK-47 has a pistol grip that makes it easy to hold. The curved magazine holds up to 30 rounds of ammunition.

rake: To sweep an area back and forth with gunfire.

Bombs rain from a B-52 above Vietnam. The airplane could carry up to 42 bombs in its hold and another 24 beneath its wings.

B-52 Stratofortress

Many experts believe that the B-52 is the most successful military aircraft ever. It was designed in the early 1950s for long-range missions carrying nuclear bombs. It was a key part of the U.S. nuclear **deterrent** during the Cold War. In Vietnam, it was used to drop conventional bombs of various kinds. After modifications, B-52s then saw service right through to the 21st century.

deterrent: A threat that deters, or prevents, the enemy from attacking.

MASSIVE AIRCRAFT

Everything about the B-52 was big. Its wingspan was 185 feet (56 m). It could carry 110,000 pounds (570 kg) of bombs. Its range was 3,000 miles (4,800 km). It bombed targets from a height of 22,000 feet (6.75 km). That was so high that often the first thing the enemy knew about a bomb was when it landed.

THUNDER

B-52s took part in Operation Rolling Thunder, the name given to a sustained bombing campaign against North Vietnam. The campaign began on March 2, 1965, and lasted until November 2, 1968. A massive 864,000 tons (785,000 tonnes) of bombs were dropped on a range of targets. The campaign ended in failure, however, because it did not force the North Vietnamese to give in.

The B-52s disrupted enemy troop positions. They also supported ground troops. From June 1965 to August 1973, B-52s flew 124,532 sorties from bases in Guam and Thailand.

B-52s drop their bombs on enemy positions from high altitude.

Ground crew load incendiary bombs onto a B-52 for a mission in February 1967.

incendiary: Something designed to start a fire or cause a fire to spread.

C-47 Chinook

Vietnam was accurately called a "helicopter war." The Chinook was the proof of this. At the height of the war, the 22 Chinook units in Vietnam were operating about 750 two-**rotor** C-47 Chinooks. The Chinook's carrying ability was key to U.S. strategy. It transported troops to locations where there were no roads, and Chinooks even carried artillery to positions on mountains. Last, but by no means least, Chinooks were able to evacuate casualties from the frontline to hospitals.

A Chinook comes in to land and evacuate troops from the frontline at a location marked by a smoke grenade.

rotor: A blade that revolves at very high speed.

A C-47 Chinook uses its **cargo hook** to bring in ammunition for a battery of 105-mm howitzers during an operation in Vietnam.

HEAVY LIFTER

A Chinook flight could keep a unit supplied for weeks with food and ammunition. The hold could carry up to 7,000 pounds (3,175 kg). Still, soldiers sometimes overloaded the helicopter in their eagerness to get supplies to forward positions. Then the aircraft could not take off.

The Chinook had one big disadvantage: Its size made it an easy target for enemy fire. The chopper had M60 machine guns on each side for protection. Flying a Chinook was still a dangerous job, however. Over a quarter of the helicopters were lost in the war.

EYEWITNESS

"I noticed there was no 'glass' in the window openings. . . [The crew chief] said 'we have no machine guns on this aircraft. If we catch ground fire. . . stick your rifles out the window openings and fire back.'"

Raymond Cochran
Naval Seabee, attached to 3rd Marine Division

cargo hook: A hook beneath an aircraft used to carry loads in a sling.

A Skyraider drops a phosphorus bomb on a target in February 1966. Phosphorus could burn skin very badly.

Bombs are filled with napalm at a U.S. airbase.

Chemical Weapons

Desperate to find ways of attacking guerrilla forces hiding in dense jungle, U.S. commanders decided to use **chemical weapons** to kill the vegetation. Other chemicals that burned at high temperatures were used to attack enemy bases and personnel. Both types of chemicals caused terrible injuries to soldiers and civilians.

chemical weapons: Weapons that cause burning, poisoning, irritation, or suffocation.

CHEMICALS IN ACTION

From 1960 to 1973, airplanes sprayed 21 million gallons of Agent Orange. This toxic chemical stripped leaves from the rain forest. It was also sprayed on crops to try to starve the enemy.

EYEWITNESS

"I have decided that the United States will renounce the use of any form of deadly **biological weapons** that either kill or incapacitate."

Richard Nixon
U.S. President, November 1969

Other U.S. bombs contained chemicals that caught fire, such as phosphorus. Napalm was an explosive petroleum jelly that stuck to the flesh. It caused horrible, deep burns. It was difficult to target accurately. Many Vietnamese civilians, including children, tragically became victims of phosphorus and napalm.

A huge explosion marks a napalm strike against suspected Viet Cong positions.

biological weapons: Weapons that use germs or herbicides.

F-100 Super Sabre

The Super Sabre first saw service in 1954 and was the first U.S. Air Force jet fighter that could fly at **supersonic** speeds. Its main job was to escort and protect other aircraft on bombing raids over North Vietnam. It took on the interceptor aircraft of the North Vietnamese air force. Super Sabres stayed in service until 1979.

As a daytime clear-weather fighter, the Super Sabre didn't need radar; the pilot located targets visually.

supersonic: Faster than the speed of sound, or 768 miles per hour (1,236 km/h).

AN F-100 releases a napalm bomb over Viet Cong positions.

STURDY AIRPLANE

The F-100—nicknamed the "Hun"—was the longest serving jet fighter in Vietnam, where it was in service from April 1961 until 1971. The aircraft were super reliable and tough, and easy to maintain and get in the air.

The aircraft could fly multiple missions every day, including spotting targets, helping in search and rescue, and dropping bombs. However, the F-100's original and most successful job was in air-to-air combat. It shot down its first North Vietnamese Air Force **MiG**-17 on April 4, 1965.

EYEWITNESS

"It was fairly easy to fly, but it could 'bite you in the rear' in a heartbeat if you did not respect it. . . The really high-time F-100 guys could make it do things that would amaze most of us."

Colonel Robert Wendrock
F-100 pilot, veteran of 280 combat missions

MiG: A type of fighter plane built by the Soviet Union.

A flame tank fires a burst of napalm at a suspected enemy position near Saigon in early 1968.

Flamethrower

By the time of the Vietnam War, the **flamethrowers** that had first appeared in World War II (1939–1945) had been improved and become even more fearsome weapons. The liquid that caught fire was now safer to handle and more effective, while the technology that shot this liquid out was very effective. In the jungles and along the rivers of Vietnam, flamethrowers were used to terrify the enemy and to destroy vegetation.

flamethrower: A weapon that sprays out burning fuel.

MOUNTED FLAMETHROWERS

By the time of the Vietnam War, larger flamethrowers were mounted on tanks or on the boats of the "Brownwater Navy." They were used to burn off the vegetation along Vietnam's rivers.

These mounted flamethrowers had a much longer **range** than handheld weapons. The fuel tanks were larger, too, so flame attacks could last longer. The flamethrowers used gasoline to burn buildings or clear away vegetation. They also shot napalm as an antipersonnel weapon.

ZIPPOS

The deadly U.S. flameboats that sailed along Vietnamese rivers were nicknamed "Zippos" after a popular brand of cigarette lighter. Guns mounted in revolving turrets shot streams of flaming napalm up to 200 yards (180 m) onto the banks. The Zippos supported land operations. The flames destroyed anything within range—but that sometimes included villages and homes.

A stream of fire shoots from a U.S. boat on a river in Vietnam. Flamethrowers cleared vegetation along the riverbanks.

range: The distance a weapon can fire and still be effective.

A soldier takes aim with his M16A1, which has been adapted with the addition of a **grenade launcher** beneath the barrel.

M16 Rifle

When U.S. troops first moved into Vietnam, their standard weapon was the M-14 rifle. This was quite long and heavy, however, and in 1967 it was replaced by the M16. This weighed 6½ pounds (2.95 kg) and was easier to carry than the M-14. It was also easier to use and to reload. On automatic, it could fire between 750 and 900 rounds per minute, up to a range of 470 yards (430 m).

grenade launcher: A wide-barreled small-arms weapon that fires small bombs.

JUNGLE READY?

Not all soldiers were happy with their new rifles. The first M16s were not suited to the tropical Vietnamese climate. The gun worked best when it was clean and dry, but it was hard to keep it that way in the jungle. The rifle got wet and dirty—and then it jammed. It was still jamming at the siege of Khe Sahn in 1968.

EYEWITNESS

"I decided that the M16 was essential, not only for the American troops but for the Vietnamese. I made such a request in December 1965."

Gen. William Westmoreland
Commander, U.S. Military Operations, Vietnam

As the war went on, the teething problems were ironed out. The gun became more reliable. Modifications like the M16A1 worked better. This could be fitted with a grenade launcher beneath the barrel. The M16 became the standard U.S. infantry rifle until it was phased out in 2010.

A Special Forces soldier on boat patrol on a Vietnamese river has a cover around the barrel of his M16 to keep it dry.

An ARVN soldier fires his M16 during a **firefight**. The Americans equipped their Vietnamese allies with the rifles.

firefight: A brief, intense exchange of fire between two military units.

M48 Patton Tank

The M48 medium tank was the largest U.S. tank in Vietnam. It had a top speed of up to 30 miles per hour (48 km/h) and was armed with a main gun and two machine guns. It was designed for combat against other tanks and to break through fixed enemy defenses, but neither of these roles was needed in Vietnam. Over 600 M48s were sent to Vietnam and were used in a variety of roles, mainly in support of infantry.

M48s of the U.S. 5th Cavalry Regiment search for North Vietnamese soldiers after the **Tet Offensive** in 1968.

Tet Offensive: A surprise North Vietnamese attack in January 1968.

M48 Patton tanks of the 11th Armored Cavalry Regiment are moved by barge along one of Vietnam's rivers.

NO TANK WAR

Vietnam was not a war for tanks. The landscape didn't suit tank combat: It was too hilly and the vegetation was too thick. The Army of North Vietnam and the Viet Cong had few tanks until late in the war.

EYEWITNESS

"North Vietnamese small arms fire was hitting the tank and flying all around me. Later, after the battle was over, I saw that my helmet had several places where some rounds had gotten close to my skull."

Dwight W. Birdwell
Tank commander, recipient of the Purple Heart

The Patton made itself useful anyway. It guarded convoys, supported troops in combat, and secured **strategic** routes. At night, tanks and armored personnel carriers (APCs) were used to encircle a camp to protect soldiers from the enemy. Pattons were also fitted with flamethrowers for clearing vegetation.

M48 tanks and armored personnel carriers (APCs) advance in search of the enemy during an operation to destroy Viet Cong headquarters.

strategic: Concerned with the overall aims of a war or battle.

In a trench with an ample supply of cartridge belts, a U.S. soldier rests his M60 on its bipod.

M60 Machine Gun

The M60 was first widely issued to U.S. troops in 1959 and continued in service with some U.S. allies into the 21st century. It was the main fire support for infantry on **patrol** in Vietnam. A crew of two or three carried the gun and its ammunition. It was heavy to carry and used up so much ammunition that U.S. infantrymen called it "the Pig." However, the gun had all-round uses and was often sited in helicopters or tanks.

patrol: A military mission carried out for reconnaissance or to maintain security.

HEAVYWEIGHT WEAPON

The M60 could be fired from the shoulder or the hip in short bursts, but the firer soon got tired. For greater accuracy, it could be supported on a bipod that was built into the barrel or on a separate tripod. It fired up to 550 high-velocity bullets to a range of 1,900 yards (1,740 m).

There were two major complaints about the M60. First, the weight of the cartridge belt limited how much ammunition could be carried. Every man in a company helped by carrying up to 200 rounds. Second, like other U.S.-made guns, the M60 tended to jam in damp, dirty battlefield conditions.

JAMMED GUNS

A major problem for many of the soldiers in Vietnam was a weapon that jammed in the middle of combat. In a firefight, this could be fatal. Soldiers complained that they could not rely on guns such as the M60 or the M16 rifle in times of danger. The U.S. Army responded by continually improving models in an effort to iron out the technical difficulties, but this wasn't always successful. Soldiers had to work extra hard to keep their guns clean.

UH-1 Hueys armed with M60 machine guns fly a **search-and-destroy** mission over Quan Rhu Tuc.

A machine-gun team from the 3rd Battalion, 5th Marine Regiment, fires on the enemy in the 1968 Tet Offensive.

search-and-destroy: A mission to find enemy positions and attack them.

The main gun of the M60 was the 105-mm M68. A Combat Brigade version used in Vietnam had a bulldozer attachment at the front.

M60 Tank

The M60 tank was sometimes called a Patton tank because it was an improvement on the M48, which was called the Patton after U.S. World War II general George S. Patton. It was introduced in December 1960 and remained in service with the U.S. army as a **main battle tank** until 1997. Like the M48, the M60 was not suited to the terrain on which the Vietnam War was fought, but it acted as firepower support for infantry units.

main battle tank: The heaviest and most powerfully armed class of tanks.

HEAVY DUTY

The M60 was far bigger than any tank operated by the NVA, but it didn't fight tank-on-tank battles. It could deliver firepower in situations that weren't suitable for airpower. It was also useful for securing roads and cutting off enemy routes.

SPECIAL TANKS

One of the most useful variants of the M60 tank used in Vietnam was the AVLB (armored vehicle launch bridge) tank. It was an M60 that carried a folded scissor bridge. The bridge could be extended to a total span of 60 feet (18 m). It was very useful, particularly in the Mekong Delta, where there were many waterways blocking U.S. movements.

The M60's turret held a 105-mm M68 main gun and a machine gun. Its sides were covered in steel **armor** up to 6 inches (15 cm) thick. It was the last U.S. tank to have an escape hatch fitted under the hull.

Commanders in a column of M60s raise their arms to warn the tanks behind them to come to a halt.

armor: A protective covering of metal or ceramics that protects something from blows.

Soldiers of the 4th Infantry Division use M79s during an operation in Quang Ngai province in 1967.

M79 Grenade Launcher

U.S. infantry on patrol in Vietnam were often fired on from Viet Cong guerrillas who were well **dug in** in trenches or under cover. Rifles and machine guns alone could not destroy trenches, and the answer lay in the M79 grenade launcher. The M79 had a distinctive sound that earned it nicknames like "blooper," "thumper," "thump gun," and "bloop tube."

dug in: Occupying well-guarded and fortified positions such as trenches.

An Australian special forces soldier teaches a South Vietnamese recruit to fire an M79.

VERSATILE WEAPON

The M79 was designed for carrying. It weighed just 6 pounds (2.72 kg), but being small didn't mean that it lacked power. It could fire grenades up to 385 yards (350 m) and was powerful enough to stop light armored vehicles. It was ideal for jungle terrain. Grenades helped to flush the enemy out from their defensive positions. They could be fired from such a long range that they took the enemy by surprise.

The M79 had one significant drawback that soldiers found maddening: It could only fire a single grenade before it had to be reloaded. That meant the weapon was useless in close-combat situations.

EYEWITNESS

"[The M79] was very popular because it was fun and easy to shoot. . . This popular weapon was dubbed 'the platoon leader's artillery.' It was a deadly little dude."

Clair William Clark II
Missileer

missileer: A soldier whose job it is to operate missiles and rockets.

M107 Howitzer

The M107 **howitzer** was sometimes nicknamed the "king of the battle" during the Vietnam War. This mobile artillery piece was used from early in the war to provide fire support for U.S. infantry. In the right conditions, it could fire a 147-pound (67-kg) projectile up to 21 miles (34 km). The M107 was a highly effective weapon.

The M107 had a crew of 13; when it was traveling, only the driver was protected by the vehicle's armor.

howitzer: An artillery gun that fires shells in a high arc to pass over enemy defenses.

A KEY PLAYER

Each M107 had a crew of 13 men. If it was driven around, it had an operational range of 450 miles (725 km). Often, however, the **self-propelled** howitzers were dug in to their positions. The M107 was used at artillery firebases throughout South Vietnam.

At the siege of Khe Sanh, a U.S. Marine firebase was surrounded by North Vietnamese forces for months. The M107 played a vital role in defending the firebase from enemy attacks.

FIREBASES

Firebases, or fire support bases, were forward artillery placements. They provided artillery support for troops far from their own bases. Originally the firebases were temporary, but many became semi-permanent. They were often in remote locations, surrounded by the enemy. Each base usually had six howitzers as well as engineers to maintain the guns and a helicopter landing pad so that supplies could be flown in.

The huge shells of the M109 were able to penetrate the thick canopy of the Vietnamese jungle.

Hidden by a camouflage net, an M107 of the 3rd Marine Division shells Viet Cong positions in 1965.

self-propelled: A gun that has an engine and wheels or tracks so it can move on its own.

ARVN crew maneuvers an M113 APC during an advance. It is armed with a Browning M2 machine gun.

M113 Armored Personnel Carrier

The M113 Armored Personnel Carrier (APC) was a valuable asset to the U.S. and South Vietnamese forces. By January 1968, there were 2,100 M113s in Vietnam. Their tracks coped with muddy **terrain** and they could cross rivers or lakes, but they were light enough to be transported by air and even parachuted into combat zones.

terrain: A stretch of land and its geographical features.

BATTLEFIELD TAXI

The M113's job was to get infantry into battle. It could carry 11 fully equipped soldiers, as well as a driver and machine gunner or commander. The vehicle could also be easily modified for any number of uses. It could carry **mortars**, machine guns, flamethrowers, command posts, or whatever was needed.

The M113 had a top land speed of 40 miles per hour (64 km/h) and 4 miles per hour (6.4 km/h) in water. It was vital for search-and-rescue missions. It was also used in most large-scale advances in the war. It was useful because it could pursue the enemy across any terrain.

EYEWITNESS

"[My M113] had all sorts of quirks, like spraying diesel fuel into the driver's compartment and using a couple of gallons of water a day. Maintenance had given up trying to find the leak. . . I simply got used to the little things and planned around them."

William Kestell
4/23rd Infantry (Mechanized),
25th Infantry Division

Soldiers head for the safety of their APCs during a patrol in hostile territory.

Infantry advance cautiously under cover of M113s.

mortar: An artillery piece that fires projectiles at a high angle.

M551 Sheridan

Although most U.S. tanks were not suited to fighting in Vietnam, the Sheridan light tank proved very useful. This amphibious tank saw service in Vietnam starting in January 1969. Weighing just 25 tons (22.6 tonnes), it could be carried by air and then parachuted into any remote combat zone where the terrain allowed tanks to be effective.

The Sheridan was light compared to main battle tanks, so it could be easily airlifted into combat zones.

amphibious: Able to operate equally well on land or in water.

An M551 Sheridan of the 11th Armored Cavalry Regiment patrols near Hung Loc in early 1971.

AN ADAPTABLE TANK

The Sheridan was not intended for jungle combat; it operated best in towns and cities. However, it proved very adaptable. Its main gun was the 152-mm M81. It fired M625 canister shells that could cut through thick Vietnamese jungle and bamboo thickets.

Some Sheridan crews rode on top of the tank. They risked being shot at, but they preferred it to being inside. The tank's aluminum armor was thin. If they hit enemy **land mines**, the tanks could easily blow up. Soldiers figured it was easier to jump off a Sheridan to fight than to be trapped inside a burning furnace.

EYEWITNESS

"If you got hit by a rocket-propelled grenade in a Sheridan turret and it got into the caseless ammunition, it was just a powder keg. The Sheridan guys kind of feared that a bit."

Charles T. Dodge,
1 Troop, 11th Armored Cavalry Regiment

land mine: A buried bomb that is detonated by weight on top of it.

A heavily armed Monitor leads an assault **flotilla** along a river in the Mekong Delta.

Monitor

During the Civil War (1861–65), the USS *Monitor* had been one of the first armored vessels to mount a revolving turret. Variants on the *Monitor* had then fought on U.S. waterways during that war. In Vietnam, where there were 3,000 miles (4,800 km) of inland waterways, vessels called Monitors came into their own again. They were heavily armored and carried heavy firepower.

flotilla: A limited naval unit made up of small warships.

MOBILE RIVERINE FORCE

The Monitor was a converted landing craft from World War II. In case of attack, it was heavily armed with machine guns, grenade launchers, mortars, and even howitzers. The vessel was heavy and strong, but its shallow **draft** meant it could sail in shallow waters.

The Monitor led the Mobile Riverine Force (MRF), which was formed in 1969. Its job was to stop the enemy from using waterways to resupply Viet Cong guerrillas in the delta. The boats opened up parts of the delta that were inaccessible any other way.

RIVER FORCE

The Brown Water Navy got its name from Vietnam's muddy rivers. The rivers acted as highways for enemy transportation. The Mobile Riverine Force (MRF) tried to intervene. The MRF combined U.S. Army troops with crews from the U.S. Navy. Its vessels included not only Monitors, but also fast patrol boats, armored gunboats, troop carriers, and napalm-firing boats.

Twin 12.7-mm machine guns are mounted on a U.S. Navy river patrol boat on the Vung Tau River.

Monitors (right, with forward turrets) are moored in the Mekong Delta.

draft: The depth of a boat's hull below the waterline.

UH-1 Huey

The main helicopter used by the U.S. military during the Vietnam War was the Huey. Its small size meant that it could land in small jungle clearings, either to fly in troops (it could carry seven soldiers and their equipment) or to evacuate casualties. It could fly low above the ground, dodge enemy fire, and could carry rockets and machine guns. It had a crew of two.

A gunner keeps lookout as a Navy Huey flies a patrol. The helicopter carried various weapons, including the M60 machine gun.

EYEWITNESS

"At 50 feet from touchdown we were met by heavy automatic weapons fire but continued on in . . . the explosion tore out the left front of the **cockpit**."

Wiliam Dismukes
Pilot, 173rd Assault Helicopter Company

cockpit: The part of an aircraft where the pilot sits.

Hueys lay a smoke screen. A top speed of 127 miles per hour (204 km/h) meant the Huey could deploy swiftly to support ground operations.

BOMBING JAPAN

The Bell UH-1 Huey—its designation was originally HU-1—transported troops, equipment, supplies, and support personnel. It provided additional firepower for ground actions and was used as an air ambulance to evacuate injured troops. It also carried out search-and-rescue, reconnaissance, and **propaganda** missions.

The first Hueys arrived in Vietnam in 1962 with U.S. Army medics. Eventually, about 7,000 Hueys served in Vietnam. The chopper was continually upgraded and adapted to meet different needs. All arms of the U.S. military flew Hueys: the Army, Air Force, Navy, and the Marine Corps.

A Huey hovers above the ground as casualties are loaded on makeshift stretchers for evacuation from the front line.

propaganda: Material that tries to encourage support or to demoralize the enemy.

Glossary

amphibious: Able to operate equally well on land or in water.

arsenal: A place for storing weapons.

chemical weapons: Weapons that cause burning, poisoning, irritation, or suffocation.

cluster bombs: Bombs that contain a number of "bomblets" that all detonate together.

delta wing: A wing shaped like a swept-back triangle.

deterrent: A threat that deters, or prevents, the enemy from attacking.

draft: The depth of a boat's hull beneath the waterline.

dug in: Occupying well-guarded and fortified positions such as trenches.

fire support: Providing additional or covering fire for forces on the ground.

firefight: A brief, intense exchange of fire.

ground-attack aircraft: A warplane used to attack targets on the ground.

guerrilla: An irregular soldier who fights using ambush, sabotage, and assassination.

gunship: A heavily armed helicopter or airplane.

howitzer: An artillery gun that fires shells in a high arc to pass over enemy defenses.

incendiary: Something designed to start a fire or cause a fire to spread.

land mine: A buried bomb that is detonated when weight is applied on top.

main battle tank: The heaviest and most powerfully armed class of tanks.

MiG: A type of fighter plane built by the Soviet Union.

minigun: A multibarreled machine gun.

mortar: A cannon that fires projectiles at a high angle.

patrol: A military mission carried out for reconnaissance or to maintain security.

rake: To sweep an area back and forth with gunfire.

range: The distance a weapon can fire and still be effective.

rotor: A blade that revolves at very high speed.

stopgap: A temporary fix for a problem.

strategic: Concerned with the overall aims of a war or battle.

supersonic: Faster than the speed of sound, or 768 miles per hour (1,235 km/h).

terrain: A stretch of land and its geographical features.

Further Information

Dale, Dye and Tom Laemline. *Small Arms of the Vietnam War.* Warriors Publishing Group, 2017.

Doyle, David. *U.S. Marine Corps in Vietnam: Vehicles, Weapons and Equipment.* Schiffer Military, 2021.

Doyle, David. *U.S. Aviation and Naval Weapons of the Vietnam War.* Pen and Sword Military, 2023.

Eyewitness. *Vietnam War.* Dorling Kindersley, 2017.

Rottman, Gordon L. *U.S. Grenade Launchers: M79, M203, and M320.* Osprey Publishing, 2017.

Skipper, Ben. *M113: American Armoured Personnel Carrier.* Pen and Sword Military, 2021.

Smithsonian. *The Vietnam War: The Definitive Illustrated History.* Dorling Kindersley, 2017.

Websites

https://www.history.com/topics/vietnam-war/weapons-of-the-vietnam-war
This website includes short descriptions of weapons.

https://www.pbs.org/wgbh/americanexperience/features/vietnam-weapons-war/
A wide range of weapons is covered, with plenty of statistics and technical detail.

https://www.bbc.co.uk/bitesize/guides/z89hg82/revision/4
This easy-to-navigate website discusses how weaponry interacted with tactics during the Vietnam War.

http://www.history-of-american-wars.com/vietnam-war-weapons.html
This site concentrates on land war weapons with a separate section on air force weapons.

Index